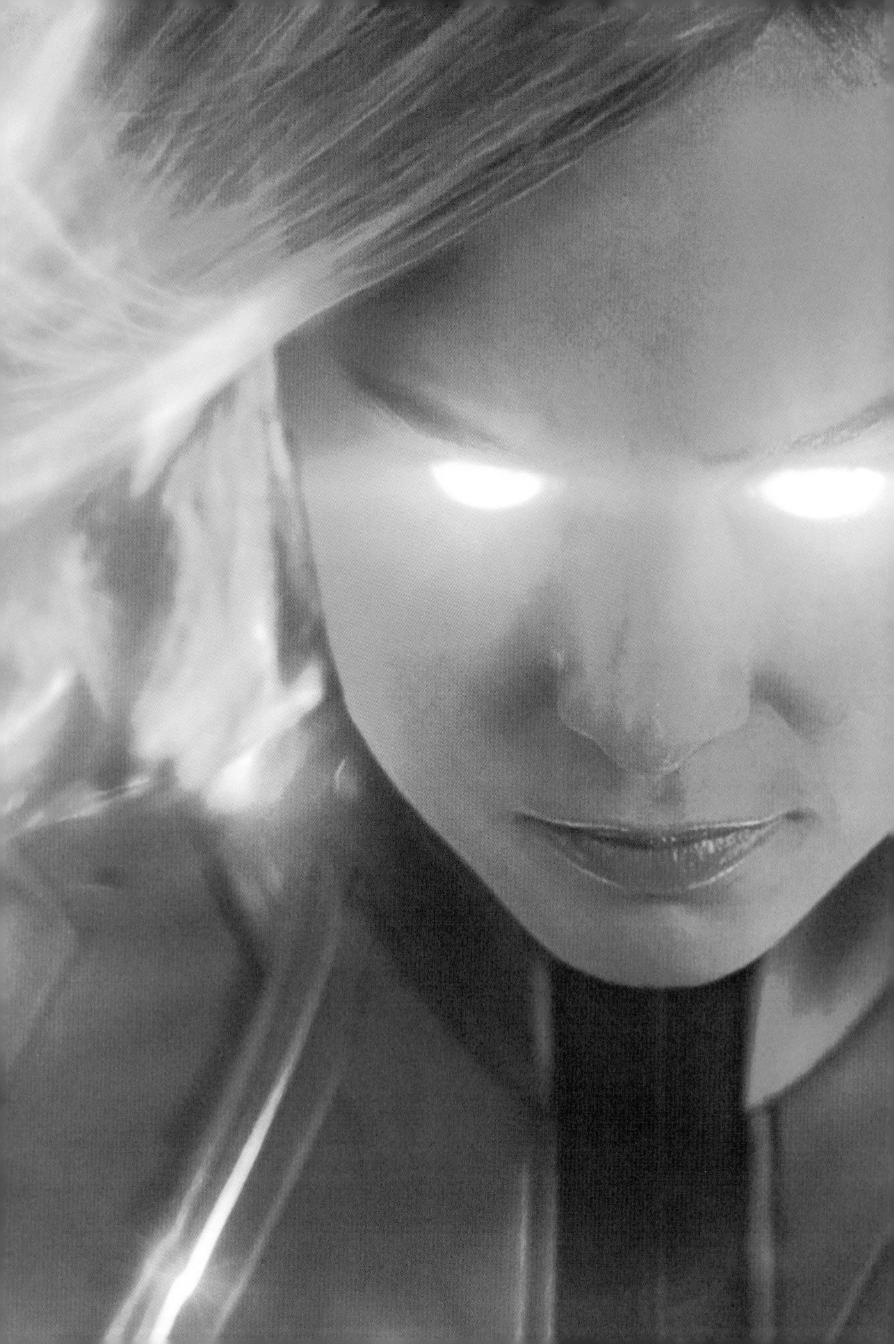

MARVEL STUDIOS

BE MORE CAPTAIN MARVEL

WRITTEN BY KENDALL ASHLEY

CONTENTS

REACH FOR THE STARS

Captain Marvel has helped and inspired countless others across the universe. Although Carol Danvers gained her extraordinary cosmic abilities from the otherworldly Tesseract, she is human, just like you and me. She only realized her full powers when she followed her heart, dared to defy an unjust cause, and accepted the truth of her past. If you seize the moment, believe in yourself, and help others like Captain Marvel does, you, too, can find strength you never imagined and become a force for good.

GO HIGHER, FURTHER, FASTER

It's easy to look at a Super Hero such as Captain Marvel and think that she's on a level that no one else could achieve. However, Carol Danvers was a hero long before she absorbed energy from the Tesseract and acquired superpowers. By following her example, you, too, can tap into your inner strength and become a hero. No photon blasts from your fists required.

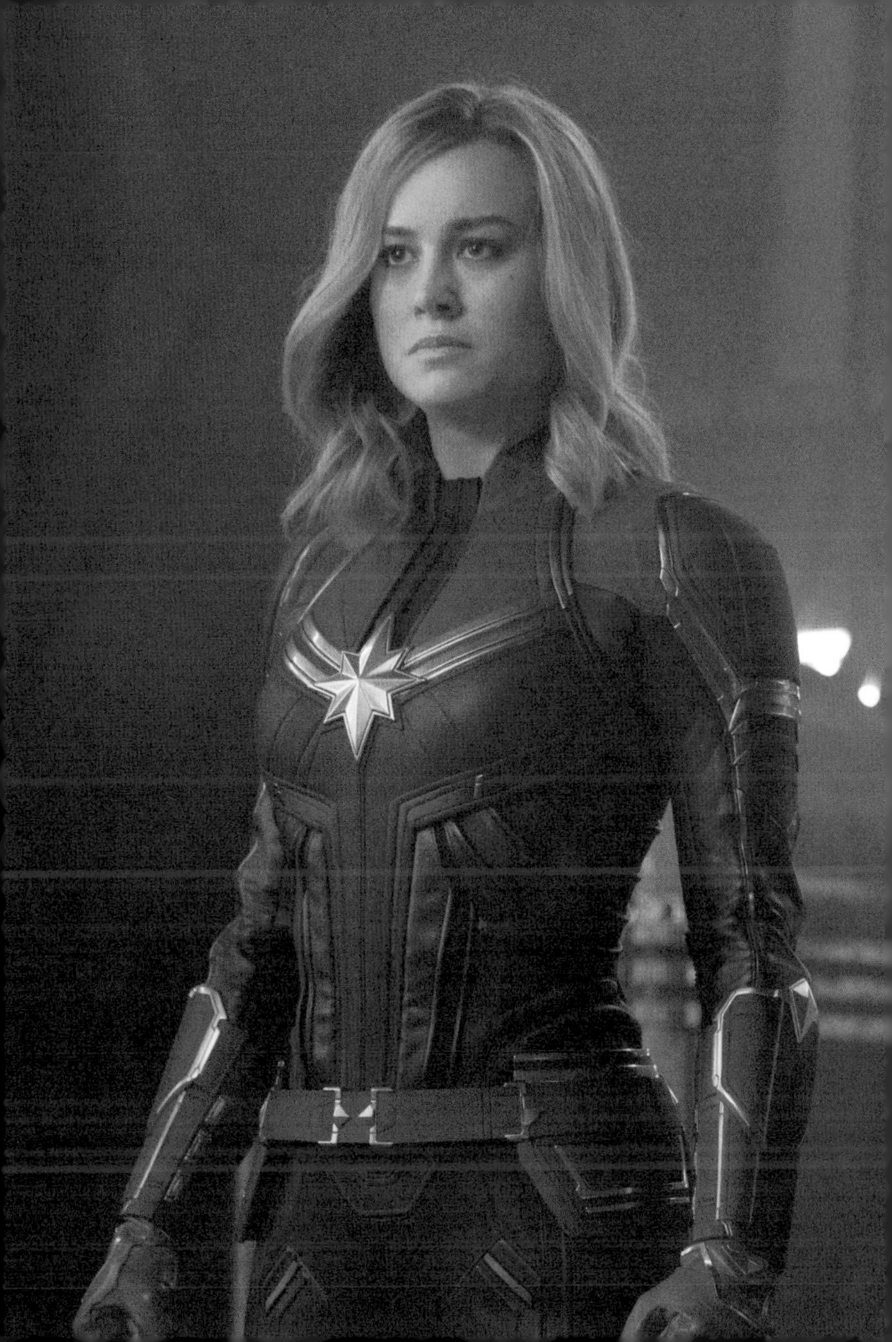

"I prefer the view from up there."
Carol Danvers

THE SKY'S THE LIMIT

Carol Danvers had an uphill climb when it came
to her dream of being a pilot in the Air Force,
but she didn't let obstacles slow her down.
Carol knew she would face setbacks in chasing
her goals, but her ambiton, courage, and tenacity
helped her to stay on course. Just like Carol,
don't let a tough climb hold you back. Aim high,
because the sky's the limit.

"You are Carol Danvers. You are the woman on that black box risking her life to do the right thing."

Maria Rambeau

TAKE RISKS

Carol Danvers never let fear stop her from reaching
a goal or helping others. When she worked with
Dr. Wendy Lawson as a test pilot, Carol didn't hesitate
to volunteer for risky missions, especially when lives
were at stake – including her own. She had the
resolve and skills to help, and the risk was worth it.
Like Carol, be smart about the adventures you
embark on, but never let a challenge keep you from
following your heart or doing the right thing.

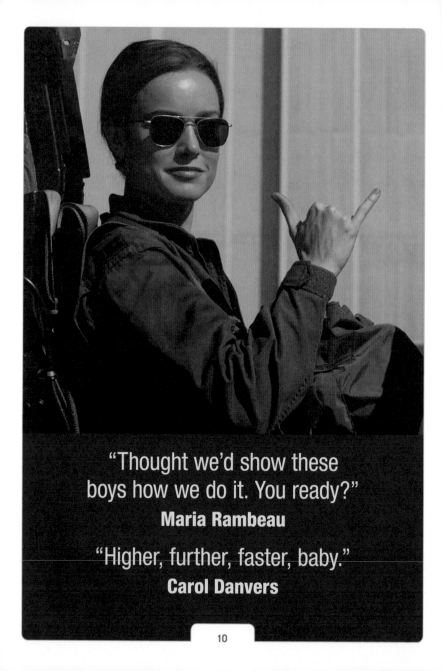

"Thought we'd show these boys how we do it. You ready?"
Maria Rambeau

"Higher, further, faster, baby."
Carol Danvers

CLAIM YOUR SPOT

Maria Rambeau and Carol Danvers dreamed of becoming Air Force pilots, but there weren't many opportunities for women to achieve that at the time. Instead of giving up and doing something else, Maria and Carol worked hard and made a spot for themselves. They didn't let outdated conventions stifle their spirit. You, too, can challenge tired traditions and pursue your goals with resolve.

"Call me young lady again, and I'm gonna put my foot in a place it's not supposed to be."

Maria Rambeau

STAND UP FOR YOURSELF

It's scary to enter a place where you feel like an
outsider, and it's even scarier to stand your ground
when faced with patronizing attitudes or knee-jerk
negativity from others. Having struggled to achieve her
cherished ambition to be an Air Force pilot, Maria
Rambeau wasn't about to let anyone talk down to her
or ridicule her achievements, and you shouldn't either.
Never be afraid to speak up for yourself, even if
you don't intend to act on your bluff.

"You're right. I'm only human."
Captain Marvel

ALWAYS GET BACK UP

Carol Danvers put her heart and soul into everything she did, but even she didn't always get it right. She failed, became disheartened, and at times felt crushed. After all, she was only human. But she always got back up. That's where her power lay – in her humanity – as the Kree Supreme Intelligence found out the hard way. You're going to fall and miss the mark, but it should make you get back up and try again.

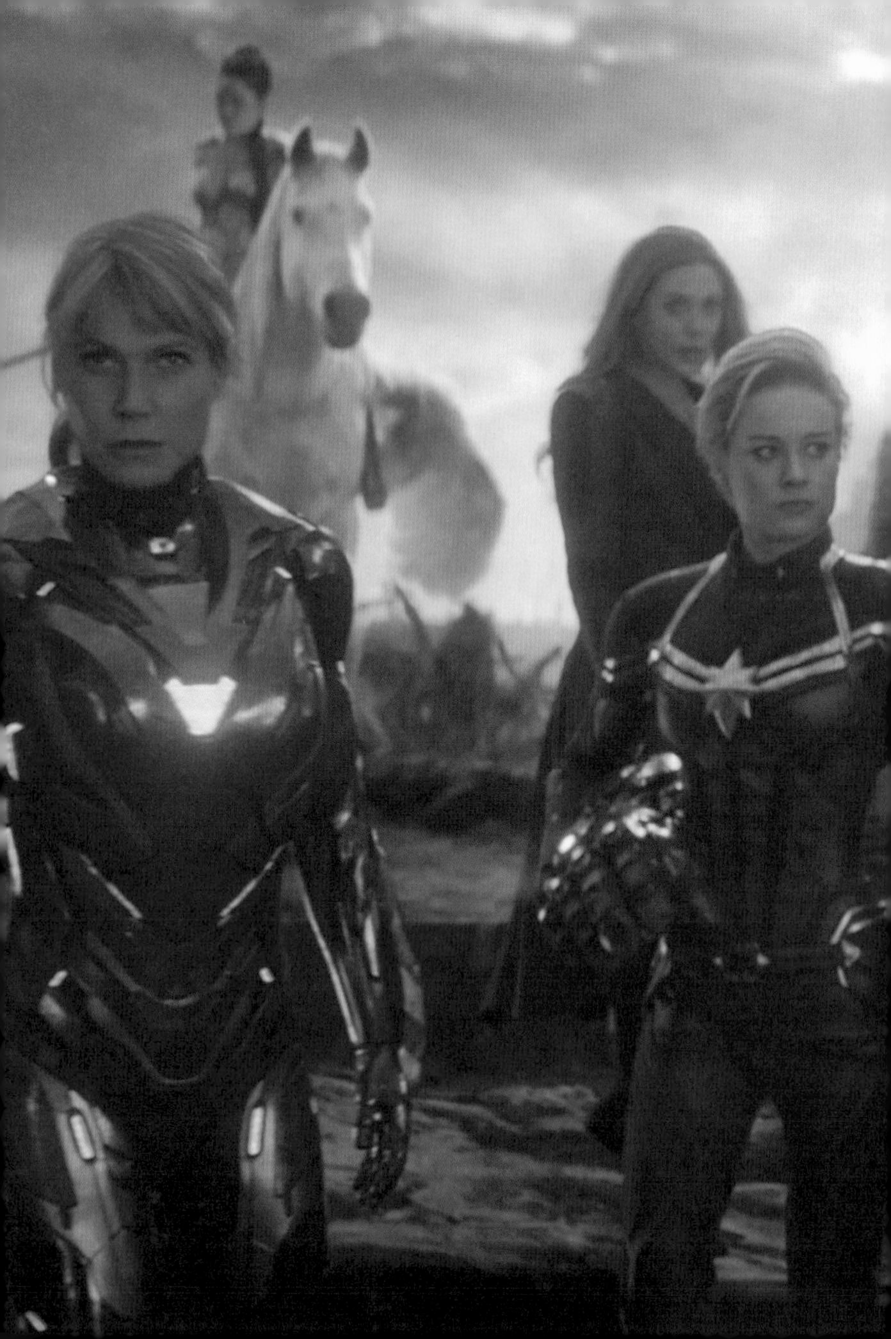

DON'T GO IT ALONE

Super Heroes rarely work alone. Take it from the Avengers: there is strength in numbers. So it's important to find others who can support you and build a group of like-minded people who have your back. Heroes know that they do the most good when they join forces to take on seemingly insurmountable problems together. So, forget the solo act and gather your team!

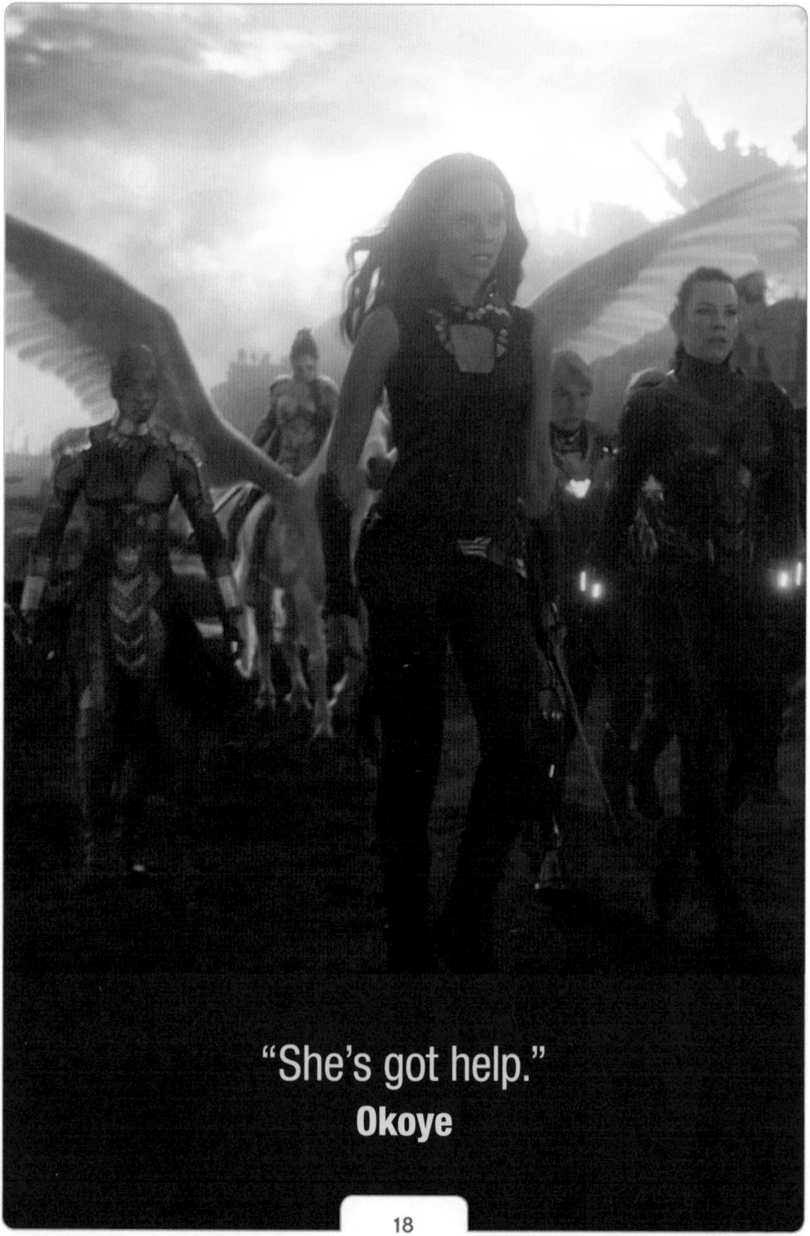

“She’s got help.”
Okoye

WE ARE STRONGER TOGETHER

It's easy to think of heroes as lone champions facing evil on their own and carrying the weight of the world on their shoulders. In reality, the opposite is true. Real heroes are always ready to support allies, as Captain Marvel found when she took possession of the Infinity Gauntlet in the war with Thanos and his army. Remember, your strength is multiplied when you're part of a team. Seeking help is never a sign of weakness, and only makes us all more powerful.

"You were the most powerful person
I knew, way before you could shoot
fire from your fists."
Maria Rambeau

A TRUE ALLY IS AN HONEST ONE

When Maria Rambeau was reunited with her long-lost best friend Carol Danvers, she saw Carol struggling with her identity and deciding who to trust. When Carol needed her most, Maria proved to be a real friend, firmly reminding Carol of her innate courage and strength. Maria always believed in Carol and wasn't going to let her give in to self doubt. A true ally is someone who cares enough about you to tell you hard truths.

"I didn't want to steal your thunder."
Carol Danvers to Nick Fury

LET OTHERS SHINE

We all have our strengths and our weaknesses, but
when we work together we should reassure and
support one another. Captain Marvel can easily blast
her way into a locked room unaided, but she lets her
new S.H.I.E.L.D. ally show off his skills as a sign
of encouragement. When you are completely
confident in your abilities, you can afford to
step aside and allow others to shine.

"Mom said we became your real family."
Monica Rambeau to Carol Danvers

FAMILY COMES FIRST

Family doesn't look the same to everyone. Sometimes
you find it in the home in which you were raised, but
sometimes you create your own from friends you meet
in life. Carol built her family with Maria and Monica
Rambeau, while Skrull leader Talos was born into his.
But both knew the importance of families. Whether you
track yours down in a plane hangar in Louisiana
or search the galaxy to find it, family matters and
is always worth struggling for.

"What's your name? Goose?
A cool name for a cool cat!"
Nick Fury

DON'T JUDGE A BOOK BY ITS COVER

When Nick Fury first encountered Captain Marvel, he had to quickly decide if she was trustworthy. Fury doesn't go by appearances; he trusts people based on their actions. It's important to give others a chance to prove themselves, because you never know what someone is capable of. That shape-shifting Skrull might be a valuable ally, and that cute cat might actually be a tentacled alien who will smuggle the Tesseract across the galaxy in her belly.

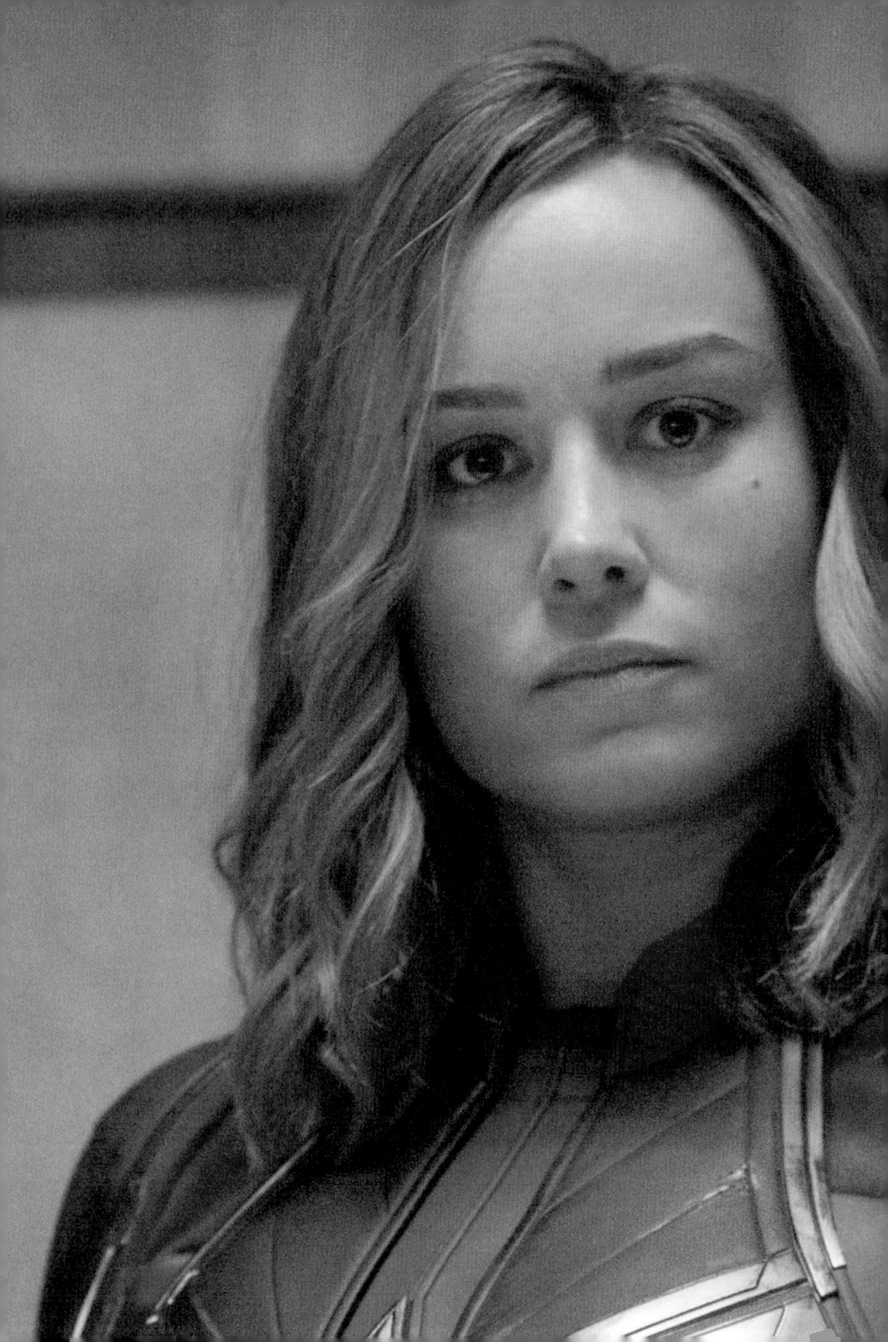

FIND YOUR MISSION

Captain Marvel has done many extraordinary things since gaining superpowers, but remember that being a hero is much more than possessing superhuman abilities. It's about using your skills and power to help others. But fighting for the right cause can be tricky, as Captain Marvel discovered when she learned the truth about her past and defected from the Kree. Her journey can help you find your mission.

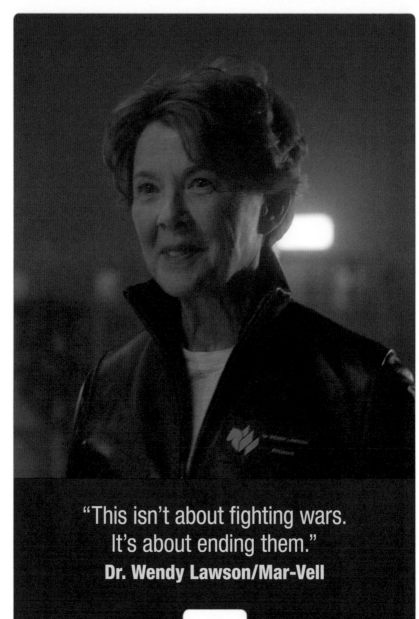

"This isn't about fighting wars.
It's about ending them."
Dr. Wendy Lawson/Mar-Vell

KNOW WHAT MAKES A CAUSE WORTHY

While we don't have superpowers like Captain Marvel,
everyone has skills, ideas and passions that make
them special. What's more important is how they
use their talents to make the world a better place.
Whether beginning your own mission or finishing
a task started by someone else – as Captain Marvel
did when she resumed Mar-Vell's quest to help the
Skrulls – your true calling will become clear when you
use your unique abilities for a genuinely worthy cause.

"She found out she was on the wrong side of an unjust war."

Talos

RECOGNIZE INJUSTICE IN ALL ITS FORMS

Everyone makes mistakes, and even a hero can find themselves fighting for an unjust cause, as Carol Danvers did when she found she'd been deceived by the Kree into opposing the Skrulls. Far more important is what you do after learning the truth. It can be painful when, like Captain Marvel, you discover you've been living a lie, but you can also put that behind you and start making things right.

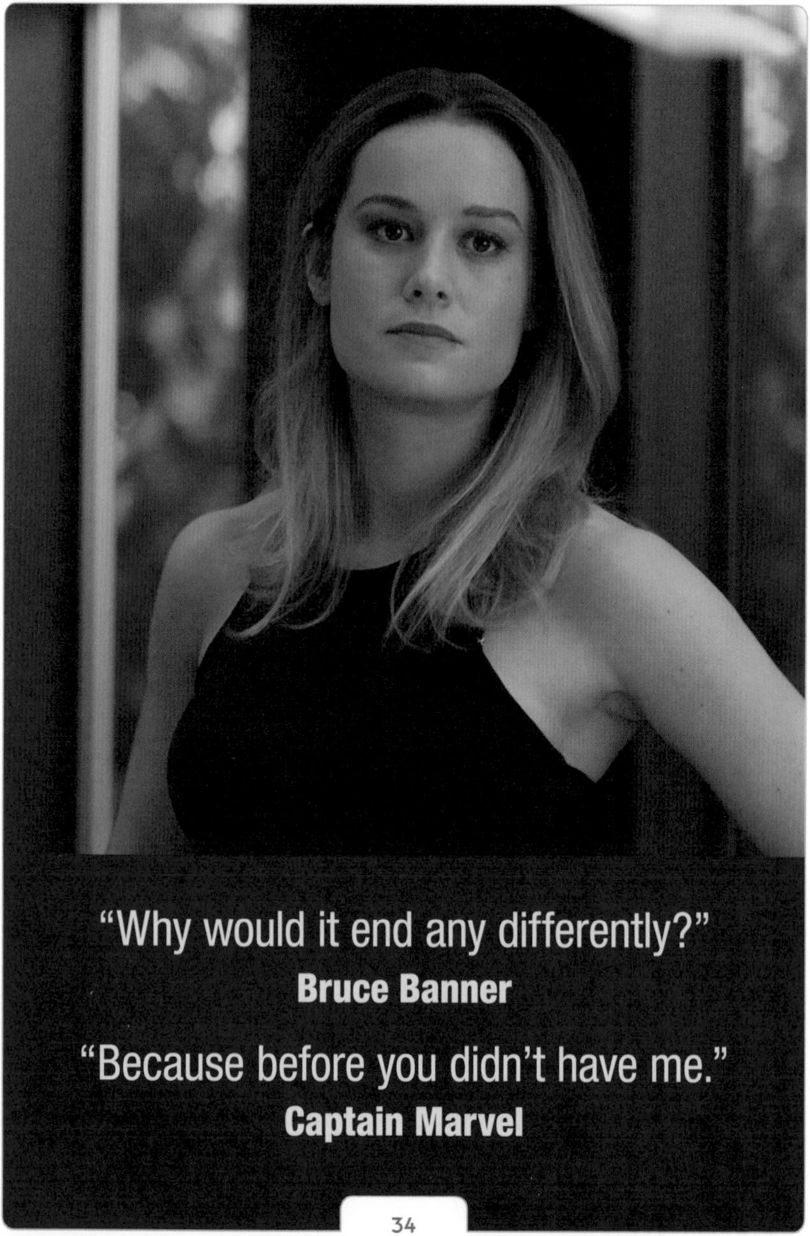

“Why would it end any differently?”
Bruce Banner

“Because before you didn’t have me.”
Captain Marvel

ALWAYS HELP
THOSE IN NEED

When the Avengers called Captain Marvel back
to Earth after the Blip, the world was completely
changed from the one she had left to help the Skrulls
find their home. With her closest friends gone and
Earth in chaos, she was determined to make a
difference and aid her newfound allies in locating
Thanos and reversing the damage he had caused.
A true hero is always ready and willing
to step up and help those in need.

"My people lived as refugees ever
since the Kree... destroyed our
planet. We just want a home."
Talos

"I'll help you find a home."
Captain Marvel

EVERYONE DESERVES TO FEEL SAFE

Everyone deserves a home where they feel protected
and safe, and no one deserves to have that destroyed
by a remorseless enemy out to gain power. Heroes
will always try to aid those in need of refuge, as
Captain Marvel did when she helped the Skrulls find
a new home world after the Kree decimated their
planet. Fighting for what's right isn't just about
stopping the baddies; it's also about helping
those who were hurt to feel safe again.

"Where are you going?"
Captain America

"To kill Thanos."
Captain Marvel

FIGHT AGAINST
ALL ODDS

Combatting evil and injustice in all its forms means
you're going to have some tough battles. But a true
hero doesn't back down because the path to victory
looks rocky. Captain Marvel wasn't afraid to take on
the mighty Thanos even after he regained the Infinity
Gauntlet, because she knew the fate of the universe
was at stake. When you find a righteous cause, fight
hard – even if the odds are stacked against you.

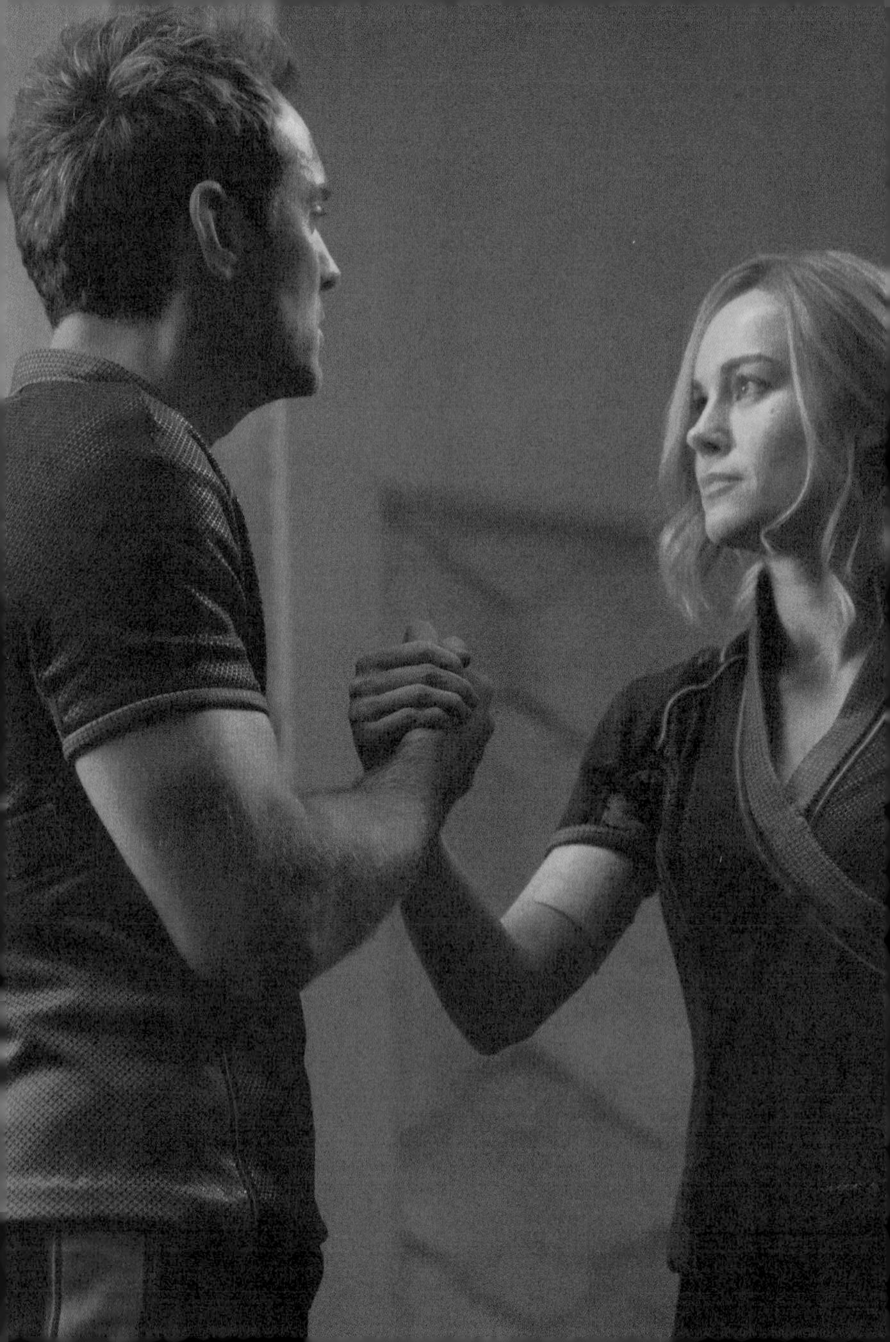

KNOW YOUR ALLIES AND ENEMIES

Every hero must learn who to trust. Discerning good advice from bad or an ally from an enemy – even one you thought was on your side – is vital. Unfortunately, knowing how to spot them is not always clear-cut, as Captain Marvel found out the hard way. But we can learn from her how to better identify the friends and mentors we should believe in, and those we should avoid.

"Danvers? We need an assist here!"
Captain America

TRUE FRIENDS CAN COUNT ON EACH OTHER

A steadfast friend and ally is someone you can
count on every time. If you have one, treasure them.
Whenever you need them, you know they will always
be ready to help. Whether you're dealing with a
personal crisis or squaring off against an all-powerful
Thanos and his army to restore the half of the
universe lost in the Blip, no problem is too big
or small for a true friend. They're always
right there beside you.

"You knew all along.
Is that why we never hung out?"
Captain Marvel

"No, I just never liked you."
Minn-Erva

YOU CAN'T FORCE FRIENDSHIP

Carol Danvers had few friends on Hala. Even after fighting alongside them, she found it tough to fit in with her fellow Kree warriors. It's difficult when you want a friendship to work but the other person doesn't feel the same way. But remember, you can't force friendship. Besides, for every Minn-Erva who may keep secrets from you, there are people like Maria Rambeau whose resolute friendship will feel effortless and even a bit like destiny.

"Can you keep your emotions in check long enough to take me on? Or will they get the better of you as always?"

Yon-Rogg

FALSE COMRADES WILL EXPECT YOU TO FAIL

Carol Danvers spent years on Hala training with her mentor, Yon-Rogg, who sought to convince her that feelings made her vulnerable. Even after Carol gained her full powers, Yon-Rogg tried to goad her into combat without her using her newfound abilities. In response, she floored her former commander with a photon blast because she realized she had nothing to prove to him. She knew that true allies will push you to be your best, while false comrades will seek to undermine you.

"I like this one."
Thor on Captain Marvel

ALLIES SEE YOUR UNIQUENESS AS STRENGTH

We all have our strengths and weaknesses, which is why we're better when we work together. An ally will instinctively and wholeheartedly understand that. They won't be threatened or intimidated by your power or what makes you different. Instead, loyal friends and allies will value your unique qualities and challenge you to be your best while remaining true to yourself.

"Without us you're weak.
You're flawed, you're helpless."
**Kree Supreme Intelligence
to Captain Marvel**

ENEMIES WILL TRY TO BELITTLE YOU

Enemies want to weaken you, but a clever enemy will not simply contradict you to get their way or make you fall in line. Instead, as the Kree did with Captain Marvel, they will attempt to deceive you, undermine your confidence, or even isolate you from those who would lend support. Disagreements happen among even the closest of friends, but belittling one another to get your way never succeeds in the long run.

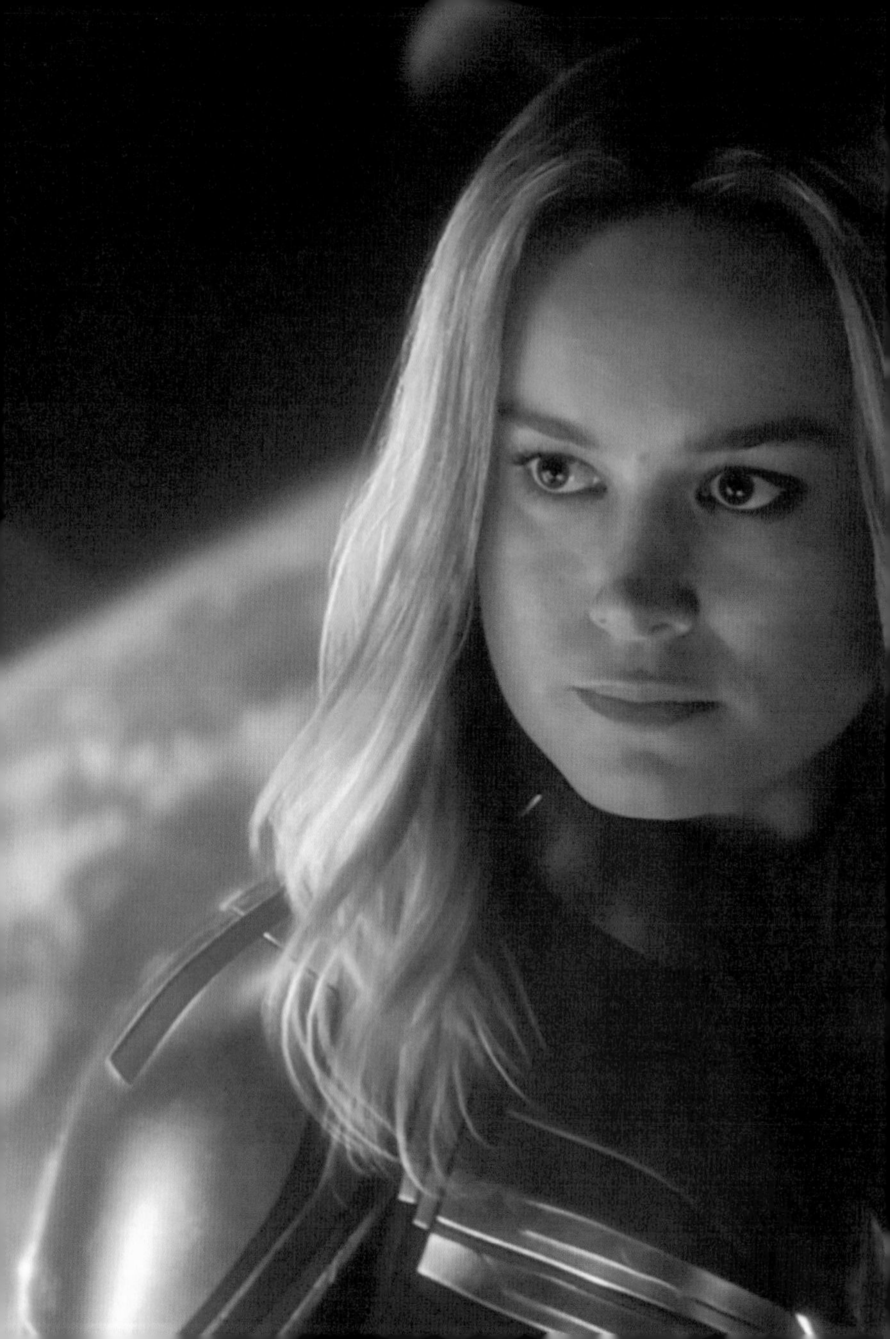

EMBRACE YOUR POWER

Stepping into the unknown and trusting your own abilities can feel scary. But becoming the hero you're destined to be means realizing you are stronger than you thought. By harnessing that strength you can do more good in the world than you could have ever imagined. As Captain Marvel proved when she left the Kree, you have to take that first step and fully embrace your power.

"I have nothing to prove to you."
Captain Marvel to Yon-Rogg

DON'T LET OTHERS DEFINE YOU

It doesn't matter how long someone has known you, no one knows you or what you're capable of better than you. During her time on Hala, Carol Danvers was tricked into allowing Yon-Rogg and the Kree to dictate who she was and define her abilities and limits. Just like Captain Marvel, when you stop letting others' unfounded criticism make you doubt yourself, you'll be amazed at what you can achieve.

"Since when is a shortcut cheating?"
Carol Danvers

"Since it violates the predetermined rules of engagement."
Maria Rambeau

"I definitely don't remember those."
Carol Danvers

NEVER BE AFRAID TO BREAK THE RULES

Some rules keep us safe and on the right path, but some can hold us back. It's vital to be able to tell the difference. Carol Danvers certainly could, before and after becoming Captain Marvel. She was never afraid to flout conventions if they stopped her from doing the right thing. When you're faced with adversity, if you follow your heart, act in the interest of others, and have the courage to break unfair rules, there's no limit to what you can accomplish.

"Tell the Supreme Intelligence
that I'm coming to end it.
The war. The lies. All of it."
Captain Marvel

OWN YOUR ACTIONS AND MAKE THINGS RIGHT

Being honest with yourself can lead to some troubling choices. You might have to oppose something you once thought was justified or make amends for a mistake you didn't realize you'd made. However, as in Captain Marvel's quest for justice, what's important is to acknowledge and own your decisions and actions – good and bad – and realize you have the power to make things right and fix whatever may be broken.

"I've been fighting with one arm tied behind my back. But what happens when I'm finally set free?"
Captain Marvel

REALIZE YOUR FULL POTENTIAL

The first time Captain Marvel was sent on a mission, the Supreme Intelligence warned her that she had to master her emotions to effectively fight for the Kree. So Captain Marvel suppressed the very thing that made her special – her humanity. It wasn't until she later confronted the Kree and accepted her real self that Carol unlocked power she had never dreamed of. Like Captain Marvel, you can realize your full potential when you embrace who you truly are.

"I'll be back before you know it."
Captain Marvel

"Maybe I can fly up and
meet you halfway."
Monica Rambeau

INSPIRE OTHERS

A hero's actions should inspire others. Being someone who others look up to is a big responsibility, so be true to yourself and put your heart into your endeavours. When Captain Marvel discovered her true power, she didn't just save the Skrulls and thwart an alien invasion of Earth. Her actions emboldened Monica Rambeau, a young girl who would become an astronaut, to join the defence agency S.W.O.R.D., protecting the world from extraterrestrial threats. In the line of duty, Monica helped save an entire town. Who knows who you will inspire one day?

Senior Editor Cefn Ridout
Project Art Editor Stefan Georgiou
Senior Production Editor Jennifer Murray
Senior Production Controller Mary Slater
Managing Editor Emma Grange
Managing Art Editor Vicky Short
Publishing Director Mark Searle

DK would like to thank: Sarah Beers, Adam Davis, Erika Denton, Sofia Finamore,
Vincent Garcia, Keilah Jordan, Tiffany Mau, Julio Palacol, Ariel Shasteen, Kristy Amornkul,
Nikki Montes, Hayley Gazdik and Jennifer Wojnar at Marvel Studios; Chelsea Alon at
Disney Publishing; and Megan Douglass for proofreading.

AVAILABLE NOW ON VARIOUS FORMATS INCLUDING DIGITAL WHERE APPLICABLE FOR THE
FOLLOWING FILMS AND DISNEY+ ORIGINAL SERIES: *Marvel Studios' Captain Marvel* and
*Avengers: Endgam*e.
© 2023 MARVEL

First published in Great Britain in 2023 by
Dorling Kindersley Limited
DK, One Embassy Gardens,
8 Viaduct Gardens,
London SW11 7BW
A Penguin Random House Company

The authorised representative in the EEA is
Dorling Kindersley Verlag GmbH. Arnulfstr. 124,
80636 Munich, Germany

10 9 8 7 6 5 4 3 2 1
001–327544–Jul/2023

A CIP catalogue record for this book
is available from the British Library.

ISBN 978-0-2415-4408-2

Printed and bound in China

For the curious
www.dk.com

MIX
Paper from
responsible sources
FSC™ C018179

This book was made with Forest
Stewardship Council ™ certified
paper – one small step in DK's
commitment to a sustainable
future. For more information go to
www.dk.com/our-green-pledge

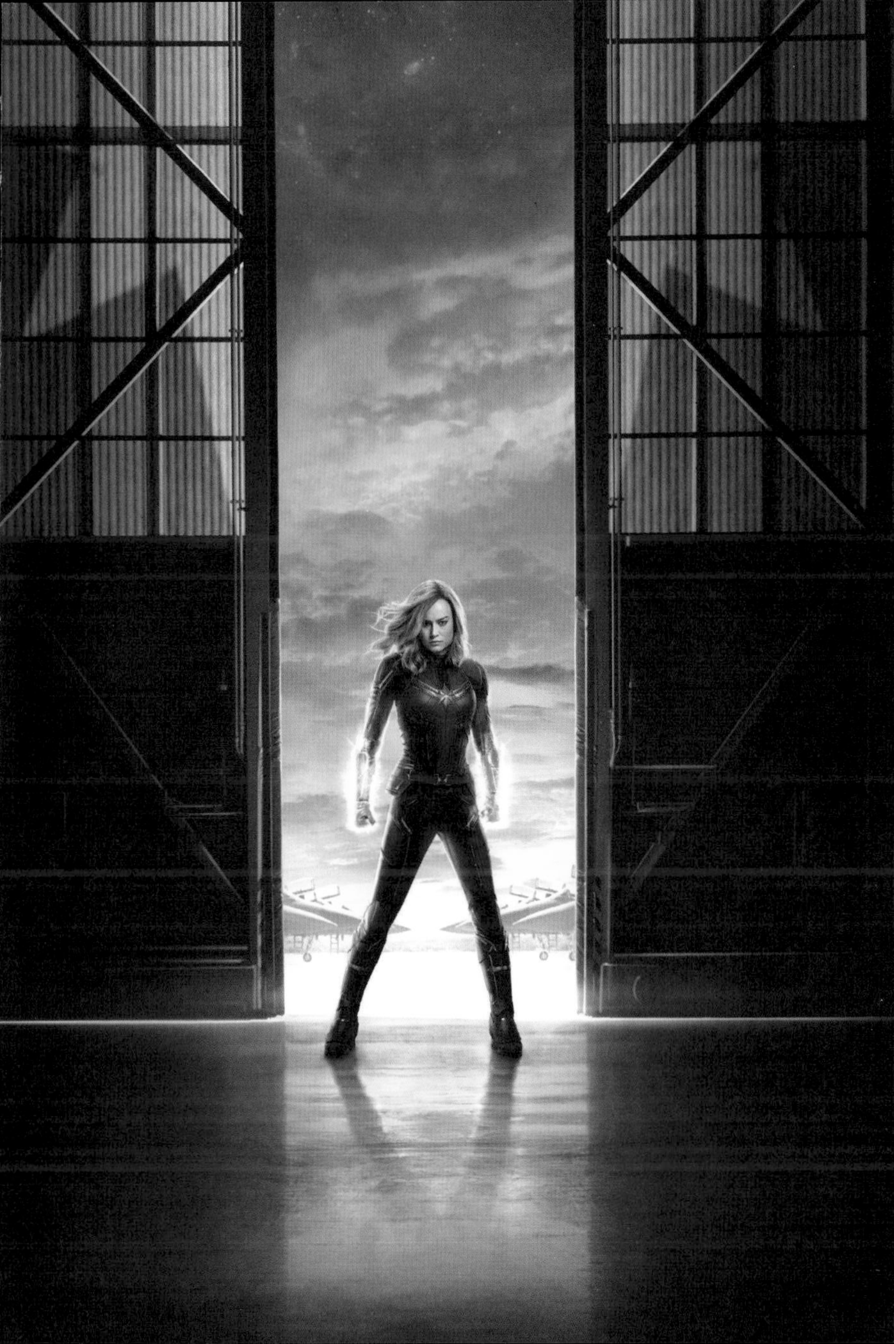